Burd

THE EMANCIPATION PROCLAMATION

". . . that on the first day of January in
the year of our Lord, one thousand eight
hundred and sixty-three, all persons
held as slaves within any state, or
designated part of a state, the people whereof
shall then be in rebellion against the
United States, shall be then, thenceforward
and forever free . . ."

—Abraham Lincoln

NEW YORK CITY

PENNSYLVANIA

OHIO

GETTYSBURG ★

ANTIETAM ★

SHENANDOAH VALLEY ★ WASHINGTON

WEST
VIRGINIA

MANASSAS JUNCT. ★

WILDERNESS ★
CHANCELLORSVILLE ★

FREDERICKSBURG ★

RICHMOND ★

RAPPAHANNOCK
RIVER

JAMES RIVER

COLD HARBOR ★

HAMPTON ROADS

APPOMATTOX COURT HOUSE ★ PETERSBURG ★

CAPE HENRY

NORFOLK

VIRGINIA

NEW JERSEY

DELAWARE

BLUE
RIDGE
MOUNTAINS

NORTH CAROLINA

ATLANTIC OCEAN

SOUTH
CAROLINA

WILMINGTON ★
FT. FISHER ★

★ ATLANTA

CHARLESTON ★
FT. SUMTER ★

GEORGIA

★ ANDERSONVILLE

SAVANNAH ★

BATTLEFIELDS
OF THE CIVIL WAR

FLORIDA

THE CIVIL WAR
AS THEY KNEW IT

ABRAHAM LINCOLN'S IMMORTAL WORDS AND
MATHEW BRADY'S FAMOUS PHOTOGRAPHS

Edited with commentary by
PIERCE G. FREDERICKS
Designed by
ANTHONY LAROTUNDA

BANTAM BOOKS

BANTAM PATHFINDER EDITIONS
NEW YORK / TORONTO / LONDON

RLI: $\dfrac{\text{VLM 8.0}}{\text{IL 7.12}}$

THE CIVIL WAR AS THEY KNEW IT

PRINTING HISTORY

Bantam Gallery edition published November 1961
Bantam Pathfinder edition published April 1966

Published simultaneously in the United States and Canada

Bantam Books are published by Bantam Books, Inc., a subsidiary of Grosset & Dunlap, Inc. Its trade-mark, consisting of the words "Bantam Books" and the portrayal of a bantam, is registered in the United States Patent Office and in other countries. Marca Registrada. Bantam Books, Inc., 271 Madison Avenue, New York, N. Y. 10016.

PRINTED IN THE UNITED STATES OF AMERICA

In this book, Pierce G. Fredericks of The New York Times has combined two uniquely distinctive statements about the Civil War: the words of the President of the United States and the pictures of the first photographer to cover an entire war. Working from the massive collection of Lincoln's papers and the enormous treasury of Brady's photographs housed in the Library of Congress and National Archives, Mr. Fredericks reveals the most memorable conflict in American history as these two eyewitnesses knew it.

TO BEGIN WITH...

Why was there an American Civil War? The men who fought it would have said that the question was whether a state or states had the right to secede from the Union. Later historians would talk of the economic conflicts between the agricultural South and the industrial North. In the end, though, the answer has to be "slavery." The other problems were certainly there, but the big one that boiled over into war was slavery.

As the Nineteenth Century rounded into its second half, America was moving west. The South was determined that slavery should move west too and the North was just as determined that it should not. Pro- and anti-slavery men flooded into the new territory of Kansas, readying for the day when it would vote to become a free or a slave state. Southerners raided the abolitionist stronghold at Lawrence, Kansas, and left two men dead. A hard-eyed Yankee, John Brown by name, struck back by killing five Southerners. In 1859, the same Brown would seize the Federal Arsenal at Harpers Ferry, Virginia, with plans for raising a slave rebellion. Marines, under a Regular Army colonel named Robert E. Lee, would march in and take Brown for hanging.

In 1860, Abraham Lincoln, who had already noted that ". . . this Government cannot endure permanently half slave and half free," won the Presidency over the candidates of a divided Democratic Party. Even before he was inaugurated, he said flatly that no slavery would be allowed to go west to the new states. In February, 1861, the frustrated South inaugurated Jefferson Davis as president of the seven states which had then seceded and the nation was on the road to a war which would last four years.

This book is the story of that war in Lincoln's words and in photographs by the great photographer Mathew Brady and others. Lincoln had posed for Brady in February, 1860, when he came to New York to speak at Cooper Union; of the resulting portrait (right) Lincoln later said, "Brady and the Cooper Union Institute made me President."

18

61

*Amid rumors of plots to assassinate
him, Lincoln was smuggled into
Washington on a closed train. There,
quavery President James Buchanan was
treating with delegates from the
new Confederacy who were demanding
that Union troops get out of the
South and surrender Fort Sumter in
Charleston, South Carolina harbor.
Inauguration Day was March 4, 1861.
Lincoln rode to the Capitol, its
new dome still half finished (right),
to make a last appeal. "I hold,"
he said, "that in contemplation of
universal law, and of the Consti-
tution, the Union of these States is
perpetual. . . . It is safe to
assert that no government proper ever
had a provision in its organic law
for its own termination . . . no state
upon its own mere motion, can lawfully
get out of the Union." Then he made
his own course unmistakably clear:*

In your hands, my dissatisfied fellow
countrymen, and not in mine,
is the momentous issue of civil war. The
government will not assail you. You
can have no conflict, without being yourselves the aggressors. You have no
oath registered in Heaven to destroy
the government, while I have the most solemn
one to ''preserve, protect and defend'' it.

*Jefferson Davis (left) was the
President of the Confederacy and he'd
never expected the job. A
Kentuckian and a West Pointer, he'd
left the army to become a Mississippi
planter famous for his kindness
to his slaves. He had
expected a military role if war came,
but now he was a chief of state—
and it was work in which he had very
little experience. Lincoln, with
his usual perception, had seen him
as the most likely head of the
deep South, slave-holding states:*

They tell us that they desire the people
of a territory to vote slavery out
or in as they please . . . It is the surest
way of nationalizing the institution.
Just as certain, but more dangerous
because more insidious; but it is leading
us there just as certainly and as surely
as Jeff. Davis himself would have us go.

Lincoln's problem was two-fold: to
take action against the states
which had seceded, but to put the re-
sponsibility for any act leading
to war on the South. His decision was
to send another supply ship to
Sumter where Union Major Robert
Anderson (above) faced Confederate
batteries commanded by General
P.G.T. Beauregard (right). A
message went to the Navy Department:

Steamers Pocahontas at Norfolk, Pawnee at
Washington, and Revenue Cutter Harriet
Lane at N. York to be ready under sailing
orders for sea with one months stores.
Three hundred seamen to be kept ready
for leaving the receiving ship at N. York.

*Major Anderson held Sumter (below)
with two companies of U.S. Regulars and
supplies to keep him going until
the middle of April. When Beauregard
opened fire at 4:30 A.M. on April
12, 1861, Anderson had, at best, only
a few days before his food would
have run out. The first shot was
good, bursting squarely over the
fort, and the Confederate gunners followed with surprisingly ac-
curate fire which burned the wooden
barracks inside Sumter. The ship
Lincoln sent did not get through and
the fire in the fort was threatening to blow the powder magazines.
On the afternoon of April 13,
Anderson, whose orders did not say
that he was to hold out at all*

costs, surrendered. There was now
a war on and Lincoln made it official:

A PROCLAMATION

Whereas the Laws of the United States have
been for some time past, and now are
opposed, and the execution thereof ob-
structed, in the States of South Carolina,
Georgia, Alabama, Florida, Mississippi,
Louisiana and Texas, by combinations too
powerful to be suppressed by the ord-
inary course of judicial proceedings, or
by the powers vested in the Marshals by law,

Now, therefore, I, Abraham Lincoln, President of the United States, in virtue
of the power in me vested by the Consti-
tution and the laws have thought fit
to call forth, and hereby do call
forth the militia of the several States
of the Union, to the aggregate number
of seventy-five thousand, in order
to suppress said combinations and
to cause the laws to be duly executed.

*To fight this war, Lincoln had an
army of 17,000 regulars, scattered
through the Indian country, and
an antique commander, General Winfield
Scott (right, seated), the aging
hero of the Mexican War. Scott had
a good head on him, though, and
he warned his President that this
would be a long struggle. Lincoln
listened—as he had listened
to Scott before he became President:*

**Mr. Lincoln tenders his sincere thanks to
Gen. Scott, for the copy of 'his views
Etc.' which is received; and especially
for this renewed manifestation of
his patriotic purposes as a citizen, con-
nected, as it is, with his high
official position, and most distinguished character, as a military captain.**

*With the calls for troops, four more
states—Virginia, Tennessee, North
Carolina and Arkansas—swung
over to join the original seven
of the Confederacy. That made eleven
Southern states against twenty-
three Northern. The North's advantage in manpower was something like
two to one overall, something like
four to one if slaves were
excepted and only whites counted.
Signs pointed to an easy victory
over the Confederates (right), but
even so early in the struggle
Lincoln saw the need to make it more
than a military conquest. He
told a special session of Congress:*

This is essentially a People's contest.
On the side of the Union it is a struggle
for maintaining in the world, that form
and substance of government whose leading
object is, to elevate the condition
of men . . . to lift artificial weights
from all shoulders—to clear the
paths of laudable pursuit for all—to
afford all, an unfettered state,
and a fair chance, in the face of life.

*As the Union men (left) came in
the regiments arrived in Washington
and it was common for them to march
past the White House and call
for their Commander-in-Chief. He ap-
peared before one such group and said:*

Gentlemen, I appear before you in
obedience to your call; not however, to
make a speech. I have made a great many
poor speeches in my life, and feel
considerably relieved now to know that
the dignity of the position in which
I have been placed does not permit me to
expose myself any longer (laughter) . . . I
thank you for the kindness of your
call, but I must keep good my word and
not be led into a speech as I told
you I did not appear for that purpose.

There was more to the war than the land, though, and, curiously, it was Winfield Scott—a soldier—who saw how it was to be won at sea. The South was poor in every kind of manufacturing. Secessionist states had taken some arms from local Federal Arsenals, but in the long run the Confederacy must import her arms or die. There was neither a Southern navy nor the means to build one. Put a blockade around

the South, said the old General,
keep foreign merchant ships from
reaching her and she will go under.
They called it "Scott's Anaconda"—
a strangling python. Lincoln listened,
called for sailors (above) and
proclaimed a blockade of the coast.

Now, therefore, I, Abraham Lincoln, President of the United States . . . have
further deemed it advisable to set on
foot a blockade of the States aforesaid.

... if any person, under the pretended authority of the said States, or under any other pretense shall molest a vessel of the United States, or the persons or cargo on board of her, such person will be held amenable to the laws of the United States for the prevention and punishment of piracy.

To make that blockade good, almost anything that would float was purchased and a few guns put aboard her (right). Even old ferry boats were armed to work the shallow rivers that ran to the coast.

Lincoln's soldiers came to Washington —led by bands, often decked out in fancy uniforms and bearing flags carefully stitched by their hometown womenfolk. The President often found himself embroiled in even the smallest details of the new army:

To Whom It May Concern: The bearer of this, Hugh Roden, says he is a drummer in the seventh regiment New Jersey volunteers, and wishes to be transferred to the second regiment New Jersey volunteers, to be with his brother, who is in the latter regiment. If it will not injuriously affect the service, I shall be glad for him to be obliged.

Then it was time to fight—or rather Lincoln was anxious for action before the militia's three month term of service expired. Under General Irvin McDowell, 30,000 men—civilians trailing along as on a picnic —marched out to face Beauregard's 22,000 Confederates at Manassas Junction. In they went against Beauregard's left flank and threatened to roll it up until Thomas Jackson won his nickname by standing like a stone wall. Then more Confederates came up to take the Yankees in the rear and the victory became a defeat and then it became a rout.

Back over Bull Run's little bridge
(left) they fled, their dead still on
the field and there were more
letters for Lincoln to write to be-
reaved parents. This one had gone
to Ephraim Ellsworth and his wife
Phoebe when their son Elmer had
been killed a little earlier in a
skirmish at Alexandria, Virginia.

In the untimely loss of your noble son,
our affliction here, is scarcely less than
your own. So much of promised
usefulness to one's country, and of
bright hopes for one's self and friends,
have been suddenly dashed, as in his fall.

In the hope that it may be no intrusion
upon the sacredness of your sorrow,
I have ventured to address you this tri-
bute to the memory of my young friend,
and your brave and early fallen child.

May God give you that consolation which is beyond all earthly power.

Out west, the opening struggle cen-
tered in St. Louis, Missouri.
The Union men rallied on
tough politico Francis P. Blair
and his rough right arm, General
Nathaniel Lyon. Lyon only had some
6,000 men. The Confederates
had almost twice that many.
The red-bearded Lyon led
his 6,000 into battle at Wilson's
Creek in August. Before the fight
was finished, Lyon was dead.
The Confederates had won the day,
but for the moment showed no
inclination to advance further. At
least the northern half of Missouri
was safe for the Union and in western Virginia, General George
McClellan won two small fights which
helped the state-to-be of West
Virginia stay in the anti-slavery
camp. Lincoln took pen in hand:

Will Lieut. Gen. Scott please consider and
inform me what can be, and
ought to be done as a recognition
of the gallantry of the officers who
fought with Gen. Lyon at Wilson's Creek?

*Clearly, a three month militia was not
going to be enough to win this war.
Congress passed a bill calling for
half a million volunteers to serve for
three years and, stung by the early
set-backs, the North hurried to pro-
vide the quota. Clearly, too, these
men were going to need proper
training. General George McClellan
(right), whose two small victories in
West Virginia were the Union's
greatest success story to date,
was brought east for the job. He
was a West Point man who had retired
a few years before the war to
go into the railroad business. When
Scott retired, Lincoln wrote him:*

**Lt. Genl. Scott having been, upon his own
application placed on the list of
retired officers, with his advice, and
the concurrence of the entire cabinet,
I have designated you to command
the whole Army. You will, therefore, assume this enlarged duty at once,
conferring with me so far as necessary.**

---

*McClellan rarely felt any need to
confer with Lincoln, but he did turn
out to be a splendid drill master.*

18

62

While McClellan drilled, another West Pointer, retired but returned to service for the war, found himself with a small command at Cairo, Illinois. Nobody thought much of the man. His name was Ulysses S. Grant (right) and there were many people who said he was a drunk. A restless soul without any very precise orders, he took his men and a few jerry-built gunboats up the Tennessee River and captured Confederate Fort Henry. Then, cutting telegraph lines so no one could tell him to stop, he turned to much more heavily defended Fort Donelson. His gunboats were knocked around, but Grant kept right on attacking until the Confederates asked for terms. He sent back "No terms except an unconditional surrender can be accepted. I propose to move immediately upon your works." Donelson surrendered. Some Prohibitionists came to see Lincoln to complain about Grant's drinking and he told them:

What brand does he drink? I'd like to send a barrel of it to the other generals.

The Union blockade was making itself felt. Luxuries were already very short in the South and far more important items would soon be too, were no way found to drive the Union Navy off the Southern ports. At Norfolk, Virginia, a young Confederate officer thought he knew how to do it and set about building a ship whose sides would be armoured with iron. In the North, though, another armoured ship was building, a tiny thing; a "pill box on a raft" was the name someone would hang on her. She was the design of an inventive Swede, John Ericsson (right); her name was the Monitor and shortly she would meet the Confederate Merrimack in the first battle of ironclads—a battle which would make every other ship in every other Navy in the world obsolete. At first, Lincoln was not impressed with the new design. He wrote his Secretary of the Navy:

I have just seen Lieut. Worden who says the Monitor could be boarded and captured very easily—first, after boarding, by wedging the turret, so that it would not turn, and then by pouring water in her & drowning her machinery. He is decidedly of the opinion she should not go sky-larking up to Norfolk.

The Confederate Merrimack *steamed into Hampton Roads and blasted the helpless wooden Union frigates. Then, with Washington in a panic, little* Monitor *(left) steamed up—almost sinking on the way—and hammered* Merrimack *back into Norfolk, never to sortie again. The President wrote:*

I most cordially recommend that Commander John L. Worden, U.S. Navy, receive a vote of thanks of Congress for the eminent skill and gallantry, exhibited by him in the late remarkable battle between the U.S. Iron clad steamer Monitor, under his command, and the Rebel Iron clad Steamer Merrimack, in March last.

McClellan still drilled and dreamed
of sailing his troops down the
Chesapeake, then attacking overland
toward Richmond. To Lincoln, the
move seemed to leave Washington
exposed; he wrote to his general:

You and I have distinct and different
plans for a movement of the Army of the
Potomac—yours to be down the
Chesapeake, up the Rappahannock to
Urbana, and across land to the terminus
of the Railroad on the York River—mine
to move directly to a point
on the Railroad South West of Manassas.

*In the end, McClellan had his way
and sailed off, complaining about the
40,000 men he had left to defend
Washington. In Yorktown, however, instead of attacking the paper-thin
Confederate defences, he set up elab-
orate siege operations (right).
It was all too slow to suit Lincoln:*

You now have over one hundred thousand
troops . . . I think you better break
the enemies' line from Yorktown to Warwick
River at once. They will probably
use time, as advantageously as you can.

McClellan stood in front of Yorktown for a month, then moved up the Peninsula, building roads (left) as he went. At Seven Pines, only five miles from Richmond, he stopped to tidy up again. While he tidied, the out-numbered Confederates of Joe Johnston attacked during a drenching rain storm. Back reeled McClellan and though he counterattacked to regain the position, the drill master began to have severe doubts about whether he really had enough men to get on to Richmond after all. His task was not made lighter by Lincoln who was worried about a threat to Washington from Confederates in the Shenandoah Valley.

I think the time is near when you must either attack Richmond or give up the job and come to the defence of Washington. Let me hear from you instantly.

*To make McClellan yet unhappier, he
had with him the detective Allan
Pinkerton (left). Pinkerton, founder
of one of the first detective
agencies in America, had known
McClellan in the railroad business
and followed him east when he became commander of the army. A good
detective, he was something less than
the ideal military intelligence op-
erative. He had, in fact, almost
a genius for seeing two Confederates where but one existed and
McClellan, already groggy from
Johnston's blow, was only too willing
to believe his agent's report that
some 200,000 of the enemy
stood between him and his goal.*

By far the worst misfortune to befall McClellan was a wound Joe Johnston received at the Battle of Seven Pines. To replace him, the Confederacy chose Robert E. Lee (right). He was considered the finest officer in the pre-war army; indeed, he had been offered command of the Union forces, but had decided to go with his home state of Virginia.
He took over with a crisis before him. Lincoln had wired McClellan:

Stripped bare, as we are here, it will be all we can do to prevent them from crossing the Potomac ... Please understand this and do the best you can with the force you have.

Now Lincoln relented and was about to send another 40,000 men. Lee had to create a diversion to hold the men near Washington. Promptly, he sent one more division to Stonewall Jackson in the Shenandoah Valley and told him to raise the devil there.

The stern Jackson (right) did not have to be told twice. Using his out-numbered men as "foot cavalry," he raced them through the Valley so quickly that the three Union forces sent against him were smashed individually before they were able to assemble. He simply out-ran them while Lincoln urged his own field commanders to show a little of the same speed—which they did not.

I think the evidence now preponderates that Ewell and Jackson are still about Winchester. Assuming this, it is, for you, a question of legs. Put in all the speed you can.

Lee had weakened himself to support the Valley, but McClellan sat on the marshy Peninsula (below), complained and received a wire from Washington:

Your three dispatches . . . suggesting
the probability of your being overwhelm-
ed by 200,000, and talking of where
the responsibility will belong
pains me very much. I give you all I can.

Jackson raced down from the Valley to join Lee. Quickly, Lee struck, trying to cut McClellan off from his line of supply. The victory was incomplete, but it alarmed Lincoln:

Save the Army—first, where you are, if you can, and secondly by removal if you must. P.S. If, at any time, you feel able to take the offensive, you are not restrained from doing so.

*Lee struck again, but it served only
to push McClellan up against the
James River where he could be supported by supply ships. On a
crest along the river, the Union
artillery (above) took position, the
guns almost hub to hub. The Confederates went in with a rebel yell,
but the Union batteries blew them
away almost before they were started.
The Peninsula campaign was over.*

If the news for the Confederacy was good at Richmond, it was bad elsewhere. The Union Navy had taken a semi-retired admiral named David Glasgow Farragut (left) out of mothballs and sent him against New Orleans. The greatest port of the Confederacy was defended by a fleet and by forts along its channel. Farragut shot the fleet to bits and his mortar boats (over page) beat down the forts. The blockade that was throttling the Confederacy was that much tighter. More and more the hope of the South lay in some brilliant success which would encourage intervention from Europe.

A jubilant Lincoln wrote to Congress

I submit, herewith, a list of naval
officers who commanded vessels in the recent brilliant operations of the
squadron commanded by Flag-Officer

Farragut, which led to the capture of
Forts Jackson and St. Phillip, city
of New Orleans and the destruction of
rebel gunboats, rams etc. in April, 1862.
For their services and gallantry on
those occasions I cordially recommend
that they should, by name, receive
a vote of thanks from the Congress.

*And out west, Confederate Albert
Sidney Johnston (right) led 40,000
men against Grant who had come up
the Tennessee River to Shiloh. Grant
was having a bad day—his forces
were dispersed and his pickets were
nodding. Johnston gained a complete
surprise in an April Sunday dawn attack,
and the Northerners were sent reeling
back to the river bank. Grant just
managed to hold on; Johnston fell
mortally wounded and night came. The
next morning, Grant's reserve came
up. Two gunboats pounded the Confederate flank and drove them
from the field. The losses were
10,000 men on each side. Lincoln
began to take notice of this Grant:*

I congratulate you and all concerned on your
recent victories. How does it all sum up?

Slowly, a Union army was coming into being. Its officers were learning their business and were getting troops—battle toughened men and boys (right) of whom the South could no longer say that one Confederate was worth two—or four— or however many you like—Yankees.

---

*To forestall a second Valley cam-
paign Lincoln called General John
Pope (right) from the west. Pope fought
at Manassas and Lee ran circles
around the bewildered newcomer.
Lincoln sent out frustrated telegrams:*

Do you hear any thing from Pope?

What news from the front?

Any news from Gen. Pope?

What news?

Please send me the latest news.

---

*Before long, Pope was back in Wash-
ington, glad to have saved his skin,
and Lee was preparing to move north
for the big win the South so badly
needed to get foreign recognition.*

Lee planned to move north behind the Shenandoah ridges, heading for Hagerstown, Maryland, then turning through one of the mountain passes to fall on the unsuspecting Union army as it came out from Washington to give pursuit. On the way up, he detailed Stonewall Jackson to capture the Northern garrison at Harpers' Ferry (right), and then rejoin. Lincoln tried to get news from frightened Governor Curtin of Pennsylvania:

Please tell me at once, what is your latest news from, or towards, Hagerstown or of the enemies movements in any direction.

*McClellan came racing up from
the Peninsula and Lincoln wired:*

Your despatches of today received. God
bless you, and all with you.
Destroy the rebel army, if possible.

And to worried Governor Curtin went:

Since telegraphing you, despatch from
Gen. McClellan, dated 7 o'clock this morning. Nothing of importance happened to

him yesterday. This morning he was
up with the enemy at Sharpsburg, and
waiting for a heavy fog to rise.

*And before McClellan lay an oppor-
tunity which rarely comes to any general. A copy of Lee's order detach-
ing Jackson had been captured by
Union cavalry. McClellan knew his foe
was divided. He could destroy the halves
separately if he got into action (above)
as fast as Stonewall Jackson would have.*

McClellan dawdled north for a whole
day. Lee, finding the Yankees close
behind, set his men at Sharpsburg,
behind Antietam Creek and sent
word for Jackson to come running.
McClellan dawdled another day, Jackson came up and when McClellan
finally attacked on the morning of
September 17, he hit the northern end
of Lee's line only. Through the
morning they battled with dreadful
losses on both sides. With a little
more pressure, the Southerners
might have broken; but there was no
extra pressure, and the
line held. Not until mid-afternoon
did the southern end of the Union
line attack. Across Antietam Bridge
(right) they storm.d. Earlier
in the day, it would have made all
the difference. So late, it was simply a gallant charge instead of the
making of a decisive victory.
Still, Lee had to fall back across
the Potomac, the victory he so badly
needed still far out of reach.

The fallen lay around Antietam Bridge, in Bloody Lane and in the fields near the Dunker Church (above). In all, the North lost 12,000 men, the South 11,000. Not only Lee had needed this battle; Lincoln too had been waiting for a victory and Antietam seemed to be near enough to the real thing. It was his intention

to give some meaning to this
slaughter and he had wanted the victory so that the deed would not
seem an act of weakness. Now, to
give the North and the world a sym-
bol of what the war was about, he
sat down and wrote the first
draft of the Emancipation Proclamation
which would set the Negro free:

I, Abraham Lincoln . . . hereby proclaim
that it is my purpose, upon the next meet-
ing of Congress to again recommend
the adoption of a practical measure tendering pecuniary aid to the free acceptance
or rejection of all slave-states so-called,
the people whereof may not then be in
rebellion against the United States,
and which States may then have voluntarily
adopted, or thereafter may voluntarily
adopt, immediate, or gradual abolishment
of slavery within their respective limits.

. . . that on the first day of January in the year of
our Lord, one thousand eight hundred
and sixty-three, all persons held as
slaves within any state, or designated part
of a state, the people whereof shall then
be in rebellion against the United
States, shall be then, thenceforward
and forever free . . .

He then went to camp to talk with McClellan (left) and from the wires that follow, displeasure is clear:

You remember my speaking to you of what I called your over-cautiousness. Are you not over-cautious when you assume that you can not do what the enemy is constantly doing? Should you not claim to be at least his equal in prowess and act upon the claim?

And later:

I have just read your despatch about sore tongued and fatigued horses. Will you pardon me for asking what the horses of your army have done since the battle of Antietam that fatigue anything?

The note about the horses may very well have been a reference to Jeb Stuart (left), the plumed knight of the Confederacy, whose cavalry rode around the Union men, be-deviled their supply trains and fought brilliantly to delay the Union advance on Antietam until Jackson and his men could get back into the battle line. Later on, Lincoln said flatly:

Stuart's cavalry outmarched ours, having certainly done more marked service on the Peninsula, and everywhere since.

And so the Army of the Potomac got a new commander—General Ambrose Burnside (left)—and the army which had not been lucky in its leaders now had the worst. It was Burnside's notion that he could run quickly down the Rappahannock River, jump across before Lee knew he was there, and charge towards Richmond. Not surprisingly, when Burnside got on the river in December, Lee was opposite him and busily entrenching on Marye's Heights behind the town of Fredericksburg. There was no bridge over the river, but Burnside expected to build one— while Lee presumably just sat quietly.

Lincoln talked to Burnside about
Fredericksburg (below) and then wired
to General Henry "Old Brains" Halleck:

I have just had a long conference with
Gen. Burnside. He believes that Gen. Lee's
whole army, or nearly the whole of it
is in front of him, at and near Fredericksburg. Gen. B. says he could take into

battle now any day, about, one hundred
and ten thousand men, that his army is in
good spirit, good condition, good
morale, and that in all respects he is
satisfied with officers and men; that he
does not want more men with him, because
he could not handle them to advantage,
that he thinks he can cross the
river in the face of the enemy and drive
him away, but that, to use his
own expression, it is somewhat risky.

Incredibly, Burnside tried to do it.
With his artillery (above) pounding
the town and ridge behind to
neutralize Confederate fire, a bridge
was pushed across the river. The
men in blue went over, through Fredericksburg and then started up
Marye's Heights. The slaughter was
terrible. In a few hours, the Army of
the Potomac had lost 13,000 men and
was back on its own side of the
river. It had never had a chance.

*Lincoln saw the casualty lists
(right) and wrote a "Congratulations
To The Army of the Potomac" which
must have struck the men in
the ranks as ironic—or even worse:*

I have just read your Commanding General's
preliminary report of the battle of
Fredericksburg. Although you were not
successful, the attempt was not an error,
nor the failure other than an accident.
The courage with which you, in an open
field, maintained the contest against
an entrenched foe, and the consummate
skill and success with which you crossed
and recrossed the river, in the face
of the enemy, show that you possess all
the qualities of a great army, which will
yet give victory to the cause of the
country and of popular government. Con-
doling with the mourners of the dead,
and sympathizing with the severely
wounded, I congratulate you that the number of both is comparatively so small.

*Again, the Union news was better from
the west than the east. Farragut had
one end of the Mississippi bottled up
at New Orleans. Now, from the other
end of the river, gun boats (above)
were poking their way downstream. They
were strange little craft with very shallow draft to get over the river sand
bars, and with armour so light that
most of the men who sailed them called
them "tinclads." First, the Carondelet*

dashed past the Confederate's for-
tified Island Number Ten and then
pecked away at the batteries below
to give the Union the river down to
the Tennessee border. Then the South
put together a fleet to fight at
Memphis, Tennessee, and the gunboats
and some rams whipped it. Now the
river was Union to the Mississippi
state line, and the Confederacy was in
danger of being cut right in two.

18

63

The Army of the Potomac spent a miserable winter (right) camped on the Rappahannock. From time to time, Burnside took them for a march in the mud, still hoping to surprise Lee. Neither the troops nor the President thought much of the maneuver. Lincoln wrote Halleck for advice:

Gen. Burnside wishes to cross the Rappahannock with his army, but his Grand Divisions Commanders oppose the movement. If in such a difficulty as this you do not help, you fail me precisely in the point for which I sought your assistance ... gather all the elements for forming a judgement of your own; and then tell Gen. Burnside that you do approve, or that you do not approve his plan. Your military skill is useless to me, if you will not do this.

The army had clearly lost faith in
Burnside; there had to be a new chief.
This time it was Fighting Joe
Hooker (right) and as spring came,
he had a plan. The Union cavalry was
to go west of Chancellorsville to
worry the Confederates. Then one
Union corps would cross the river
again at Fredericksburg to draw Lee
that way. Once he was drawn, the rest
of the Union army would leap over
the river near Chancellorsville, fall
upon the surprised Lee and destroy
him. Lee did go toward Fredericksburg
and Hooker did surprise him, but so
slowly that Lee was able to get his
men turned around and into line.
Then Lee pulled Jackson out of the
fight and sent him on an all day
march through the woods, all the
way around to the Union's open
right flank. Late that afternoon Jackson fell
upon the astonished Yankees and
Hooker was close to losing his whole
army when darkness intervened.
Through the third day, he clung
desperately to the river bank, then
Lee turned from him to deal with

the Yankees attacking at Fredericksburg. It was a Confederate victory—but there had been a loss, a great one. Stonewall Jackson was dead, mortally wounded by a stray shot from one of his own men.

There were prisoners from these battles and those who flowed north lived about as well as prisoners ever do live in a war. The men taken south, though, went to an experience almost worse than battle itself.

The South had no desire to treat them badly, but food was scarce, there was hardly enough for the army. Men who lived through Andersonville, Georgia (below), were living skeletons when freed at the end of the war.

*Facilities for treating the wounded
were primitive and women of
both sides followed the armies
to help as only women could. The
most famous of them was a New
Englander, Clara Barton (right), who
served through the war and founded
the American Red Cross. Senator
Charles Sumner said of her, "She
has the talent of a statesman,
the command of a general
and the heart and hand of a woman."*

The last Confederate stronghold on the Mississippi was Vicksburg and U. S. Grant had been harrying it, getting angrier and angrier with the frustrating swamps that lay north of the city. Now he marched his men down the west bank of the river until they were south of the city and Admiral David Porter (left), who had handled Farragut's mortar boats at New Orleans, ran his gunboats past the blasting of Vicksburg's batteries to join him. What was Grant up to? He proposed to ferry his men to the Vicksburg side of the river, forget about his supply lines and attack the city from the south. The men could live off the country. Over the river they went and stodgier men said that this time Grant had certainly ruined his career. Instead, Grant ruined a relief force heading for Vicksburg, then settled down to a strangling siege of the city. Lincoln noted:

Whether Gen. Grant shall or shall not consummate the capture of Vicksburg, his campaign from the beginning of this month up to the twenty second day of it, is one of the most brilliant in the world.

*Then, in July, Vicksburg (above)
fell, starved out, and Lincoln wrote
Grant at length for the first time:*

I do not remember that you and I ever
met personally. I write this now as a
grateful acknowledgement for the almost
inestimable service you have done the
country. I wish to say a word further.
When you first reached the vicinity of
Vicksburg, I thought you should do, what

you finally did—march the troops across
the neck, run the batteries with the
transports and thus go below and I never
had any faith . . . that the Yazoo Pass
expedition and the like would succeed.
When you got below and took Port Gibson,
Grand Gulf and vicinity, I thought
you should go down the river and join
Gen. Banks; and when you turned
Northward East of the Big Black, I
feared it was a mistake. I now
wish to make the personal acknowledgement
that you were right, and I was wrong.

Back east, the South still needed
the big win and Lee headed for Pennsylvania again. Pleasant farm country
and sleepy farm towns like Gettysburg (above) lay in his path. Lincoln
wired Hooker to be off after him:

So far as we can make out here, the enemy
has Milroy surrounded at Winchester and
Tyler at Martinsburg . . . If the head
of Lee's army is at Martinsburg and the
tail of it on the Plank road between
Fredericksburg and Chancellorsville, the animal must be very
slim somewhere. Could you not break him?

Hooker trailed Lee north, staying
between him and Washington; but with
the enemy clearly into Pennsylvania,
Lincoln decided that the loser at
Chancellorsville was not the man for
the next big fight. The new commander,
who had had a corps, was intelligent,
short tempered George Gordon Meade
(right). To supplement his efforts,
a Presidential Proclamation went out
calling for 100,000 militia to
rise and defend their homeland:

**Whereas the armed insurrectionary com-
binations now existing in several of
the States are threatening to make inroads
into the states of Maryland, Western
Virginia, Pennsylvania and Ohio, requir-
ing immediately an additional military
force for the service of the United States.**

*Lee's men (left) tramped north and
they believed they could whip any
army in the world. Through southern
Pennsylvania they raided, taking the
shoes and food they needed so badly.
Then Lee pulled his groups southeast,
concentrating to face the Army
of the Potomac which they had defeat-
ed so often before. Meade, the new
commander, was putting out cavalry,
feeling for his foe. He had a notion
that he wanted to make his stand
along Pipe Creek, but two great
armies were coming together—75,000
Southerners, 87,000 Northerners—
and where they collided was the
place the fight was going to be.
Back in Washington, Lincoln
had been feeling a little more com-
fortable and telling Mrs. Lincoln:*

I do not think the raid into Pennsylvania
amounts to anything at all.

On June 30, General John Buford
(right) and his division of cavalry
came clattering into Gettysburg;
to Buford, this town looked like
the place where Lee's men would
come together. Heavy patrols went out
the roads running west and north,
and Buford figured he was in for a
fight in the morning. Morning
proved him right. In from the west,
came a Confederate corps—A. P.
Hill's—and the Union cavalrymen
fought, dismounted, from a ridge just
west of the town. For two hours
they held, then Reynolds' corps
came up for the Union to jar the
Confederate advance back on its
heels. It was the last good Northern
moment of the day. A sharpshooter
got Reynolds and Ewell brought
another Confederate corps onto the
field from the north. Union troops
came all through the day, but
there weren't enough of them and by
nightfall they were scrambling
back through the town, forming a
shaky line on Cemetery Hill which
Ewell might have knocked to pieces,
had he put more into a last, hard thrust.

Through a wild night, Meade got the rest of his men onto the battlefield. His right lay on Culp's Hill which faced north, his center and left on Cemetery hill which curved down from Culp's to face west. On the second day Lee planned to hit the left with General James Longstreet's corps, and the right with peg-legged Richard Ewell's corps. Co-ordination went sour and the attacks did not go well, but Longstreet's men did cut up Union politician-general Dan Sickles' corps which the eccentric Sickles had posted further forward than Meade had ordered. The bullets flew so thickly that day that the very trees were pock-marked with them (right).

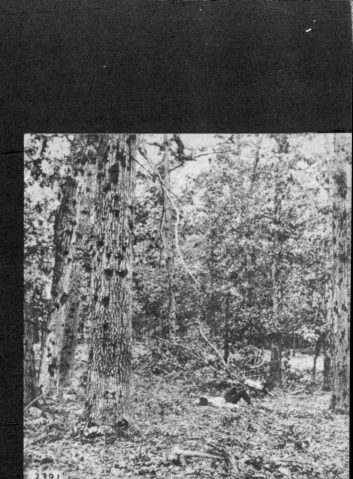

The nearest thing to a real Confederate success that day came when fire-eating General John Hood saw a hill on the south of the Union line—Little Round Top—unoccupied and sent his men swarming up it. If he could have held the hill, he could have rolled up the whole Yankee line, but Union General Gouverneur Warren organized a counter-attack. There was a hand-to-hand brawl at the top of the hill and then the Confederates were back across the way, sniping from Devil's Den (right).

The next day was July 3, 1863 and it is probably the most famous single day in American military history. Having pounded the Union wings, Lee decided that a smash at their center would go through to victory. To do the job there were 15,000 men under the command of General George Pickett (right). Legend has it that they were Virginians, but actually there were men from almost all the Confederate states present. At one in the afternoon, the Confederate artillery opened, seeking to pound down the Union guns which had beaten them at Malvern Hill. The bombardment and the counter-battery went on for an hour, then the Union guns went silent. Pickett sent his men out and before them lay a wide, shallow valley which rose to a low ridge where the Yankees lay. The Union artillery went at it again; they had shut down only to save ammunition, and big holes began to appear in the beautifully even ranks. But the Confederates marched

until they were close enough for
the Union infantrymen to join
in the fire. Then a great rebel yell
rose from Pickett's men and they
went forward at the double into the
Union line. Here and there, a
few of them broke through, but there
were too many guns and too many
tough Yankees with bayonets. Back
they went and Lee said, "It is all my
fault." No matter whose fault it was,
the Confederate States of America had
come as far north as they were to go.

*On the Fourth of July, Lin-
coln told the country the news:*

**The President announces to the country
that news from the Army of the Potomac . . .
is such as to cover that Army with the**

highest honor, to promise a great
success to the cause of the Union, and
to claim the condolence of all for
the many gallant fallen. And that for
this, he especially desires on this day,
He whose will, not ours, should ever
be done, be everywhere remembered and
reverenced with profoundest gratitude.

The decisive victory, the smashing of
the Army of Northern Virginia for
which Lincoln had hoped, was not to be.
Lee made his way back south and
Meade was not the man to follow him
hard enough to get in a death blow.
Still, the South faced the
future knowing that it had missed

*the big victory, the victory it
had to have to win English support,
knowing that it was cut in two
along the line of the Mississippi,
knowing that every day the
blockade was getting tighter. There
would be two more years of war, but
night was settling on the Confederacy.*

The casualties were enormous. Lee had some 28,000 killed and wounded, Meade 23,000. For the Union men, there were at least the crude hospitals (below) near the field. One who survived them said later, "It was dark and the building lighted partially with candles. All around . . . lay the wounded men, some cursing and swearing and some praying; in the middle of the room there was some 10 or 12 tables with just

*enough to lay a man on; these were
used as dissecting tables and
they were covered with blood . . . By
the side of the tables was a heap
of feet, legs and arms. On one
of these I was laid and . . . (the
surgeon) felt in my mouth and then
wanted to give me chloroform; this
I refused to take and he took a pair
of scissors and cut out the pieces
of bone in my mouth; then gave me a
drink of whiskey and had me laid away."*

For the Union dead, there was to be a great national cemetery on the battlefield. By November, it was ready to be dedicated and Abraham Lincoln went down to sit in the late fall chill while the crowd (left) listened to a two hour address by the foremost platform artist of the day, Mr. Edward Everett. It had been known, that Mr. Everett would be lengthy, hence Lincoln had kept his own remarks brief. When Everett finished, he rose to deliver them. If Gettysburg is our most famous battle, no less are Lincoln's remarks our most famous presidential utterance.

Four score and seven years ago, our fathers brought forth on this continent, a new nation, conceived in Liberty and dedicated to the proposition that all men are created equal.

Now we are engaged in a great civil war, testing whether that nation or any nation so conceived and so dedicated, can long endure. We are met on a great battlefield of that war. We have come to dedicate a portion of that field, as a final resting place for those who here gave their lives that that nation might live. It is altogether fitting and proper that we should do this.

But, in a larger sense, we can not dedicate—we can not consecrate—we can not hallow—this ground. The brave men, living and dead, who struggled here, have consecrated it, far above our poor power to add or detract. The world will little note, nor long remember, what we say here, but it can never forget what they did here. It is for us the living, rather, to be dedicated here to the unfinished work which they who fought here have thus far so nobly advanced. It is rather for us to be here dedicated to the great task remaining before us—that from these honored dead we take increased devotion to that cause for which they gave the last full measure of devotion—that we here highly resolve that these dead shall not have died in vain—that this nation, under God, shall have a new birth of freedom—and that government of the people, by the people, for the people, shall not perish from the earth.

In eastern Tennessee that summer, a
Union army under General William
Rosecrans was nosing dangerously
close to Georgia and Alabama.
Part of Longstreet's corps
went out to help send Rosecrans
reeling back north.
The armies met along Chicka-
mauga Creek in September. All
one day the armies battered each other.
Then on the second day an order
was misread, a Union division pulled
out of the center of the line, and
Longstreet's men went whooping
through the hole to send most of the
Yankees streaming back toward
Chattanooga. Only General George
Thomas (right) stood firm. On a
little ridge, he drew up what was
left of his own corps and any strag-
glers he could lay hands on.
In the end, Bragg had
the field, but at the cost of so
many casualties that he could
not strike another blow. To the north
Thomas was "The Rock of Chickamauga"
and Lincoln wrote a friend:

It is doubtful whether his heroism
and skill exhibited last Sunday afternoon,
was ever surpassed in the world.

Still, Bragg had his enemy bottled up in Chattanooga which he could watch from the commanding Missiona Ridge (below). U. S. Grant was sent along to alleviate the situation. It was no small task; Grant fancied no one could get straight up the ridge, but perhaps General William T. Sherman could get around it on the north while Fighting Joe Hooker harassed it on the south. In the center, Thomas and his men were to demonstrate just enough to keep the Confederates busy. Sherman ran into hard going. Hooker—to

*everyone's surprise—climbed all
the way up Lookout Mountain, but
the ridge still held. Grant ordered
Thomas's men forward to the foot
of the ridge—just a little diversion
to take pressure off Sherman.
Forward they went and while Grant
and Thomas gaped, kept right
on going up the ridge and over it,
while the Confederates fled. A delighted
Lincoln wrote Grant:*

**Your despatches as to fight on
Monday and Tuesday are here. Well done.
Many thanks to all.**

18

Lincoln made up his mind.
Meade would remain in command of the
Army of the Potomac, but U. S. Grant (left)
would be brought east to be supreme
commander of all the Northern armies.
In a speech when Grant arrived in
Washington, the President said:

The nation's appreciation of what you have
done and its reliance upon you for what
remains to do, in the existing great
struggle, are now presented with this com-
mission, constituting you Lieutenant General in the Army of the United States.
With this high honor devolves upon
you also, a corresponding responsibility.
As the country herein trusts you, so,
under God, it will sustain you.
I scarcely need to add that with what
I here speak for the nation
goes my own hearty personal concurrence.

And the next day there was a note to Grant:

Mrs. L invites yourself and General
Meade to dine with us Saturday evening.
Please notify him, and answer
whether you can be with us at that time.

While the armies camped and
waited for spring and dry roads,
Grant made his plans. He would attack
straight toward Richmond. Lee must
come out to fight him and once
the fight started Grant would keep
it up day after day, week after week
in a war of attrition the North
could afford far better than the
South. From the west, Sherman, now
in command, would drive for Atlanta,
destroying food, factories,
everything the South had which could
help them keep on fighting the war.
Then the men and the wagons headed
south and Lincoln wrote Grant:

Not expecting to see you again before the
Spring campaign begins, I wish to
express in this way, my entire
satisfaction with what you have done
up to this time, so far as I understand
it. The particulars of your plans
I neither know, or seek to know. You
are vigilant and self reliant; and pleased
with this, I wish not to obtrude any
constraints or restraints upon
you. While I am very anxious that
any great disaster, or the capture
of our men in great numbers, shall be
avoided, I know these points are less
likely to escape your attention than
they would be mine. If there is anything
wanting which it is within my power to
give, do not fail to let me know it.

And now with a brave Army
and a just cause, may God sustain you.

Grant was moving along narrow, winding
roads into the Wilderness (left),
a vast tangle of second growth scrub
and trees in northern Virginia. Lee
let him get into the thickets and
then struck. For two days, the armies
ravaged one another in undergrowth
so thick that a man was hard put to
see more than a few feet. The
brush caught fire and wounded burned
to death. By the end of the second
day, Grant had an appalling 17,000
casualties. When Lee heard men
and wagons moving in the night,
he assumed, not unreasonably, that
Grant had made his fight, failed
to break the Army of Northern Virginia and was heading home to lick
his wounds. Not Grant, though—
he was simply sliding to the left,
going around Lee's flank and
deeper still into Virginia. At a
band concert, Lincoln said:

Ladies and gentlemen, you, no doubt
desire to have a speech from me. In lieu
of a speech, I propose that we
give three cheers for General Grant
and all the armies under his command.

157

The new battleground was Spottsylvania and for two more days there was an awful slaughter, more work than the burial parties (right) could handle. The North could replace its losses, the South could not. Grant slid left again to go further south and in spite of the casualty lists, Lincoln supported him to the hilt:

I think, without knowing the particulars of the plans of General Grant, that what has been accomplished is of more importance than at first appears. I believe I know that Gen. Grant has not been jostled from his purpose.

*Grant (below, seated by tree, head
down) stood before Cold Harbor, mis-
calculated and put in an attack that
cost 5,000 men in ten minutes. It was
a jolt, but he went on south, aiming
to get to the James River, across
it and in on Petersburg, the vital
railroad center south of Richmond.*

Grim William T. Sherman (right)
also started to move south in early
May and just before he departed
Chattanooga, Lincoln wrote him:

I have an imploring appeal in behalf of
the Citizens who say your order No. 8 will
compel them to go North ... This is, in no
sense, an order; nor is it even
a request that you will do anything
which, in the least, shall be a drawback
upon your military operations, but
any thing you can do consistently
with those operations, for these suf-
fering people, I shall be glad of.

Sherman snapped back, "It is
demonstrated that the railroad can-
not support the army and the people
too. One or the other must
quit and the army don't intend
to unless Joe Johnston makes us."

Joe Johnston (right) couldn't make Sherman do anything. The Yankees had a slight edge in manpower, but their general preferred to slip around Johnston's flanks, leaving him a choice of falling back or being encircled. Johnston fell back, saving his men, waiting for an enemy mistake. In Richmond, Jefferson Davis, who never cared for Johnston anyway, was becoming impatient. When Sherman slipped over the Chattahoochee River, the last good defense line outside Atlanta, Georgia, Davis could stand no more. Out went Johnston and in came John Hood who, if he could do nothing else, could attack like the devil himself. Sherman braced to receive him.

If Grant got across the James River, he would eventually break the railroad lines and Petersburg and Richmond would fall. It is no great thing to cross a river, but Grant had to do it without being observed by Lee. If Lee caught him with half his army on one side, half on the other, the Army of the Potomac was likely to go under in the process. Accordingly, the Union cavalry feinted north of Richmond and before Lee saw through it, Grant had his pontoons (right) over the James and his army across. Meanwhile, Lincoln had been re-nominated for the presidency and to some visiting well wishers, said:

I suppose that you have done me this kindness in connection with the action of the Baltimore convention which has recently taken place, and with which of course, I am very well satisfied (laughter). What we want, still more than Baltimore conventions or presidential elections is, success under Gen. Grant.

If you had been Robert E. Lee in the summer of 1864, you might well have asked, "What am I to do?" The key to Richmond was threatened. If the city went, the rickety Confederate government would go with it. Lee had too few men to attack; he waited.

Lincoln saw the climax at hand and
wired Grant when he had crossed the James
River and set up his new base (above):

Have just read your despatch of
1 PM yesterday. I begin to see it. You
will succeed. God bless you all.

At sea, there was more good news for the President. The Confederate commerce raider Alabama, commanded Captain Raphael Semmes, had been a devil on the seas, making a hash of Union shipping. Now, the U.S.S. Kearsarge, Captain John Winslow, (center, below) commanding, had caught her coming out of Cherbourg, France and sent her down in a stand-up ship to ship fight.

Lincoln sent Congress word:

I most cordially recommend that Captain
John A. Winslow, U.S. Navy, receive
a vote of Thanks from Congress, for the
skill and gallantry exhibited by him
in the brilliant action, whilst in
command of the U.S.S. Steamer Kearsarge
which led to the total destruction of the Piratical craft Alabama
on the 19 June, 1864—a vessel
superior in tonnage, superior in number
of guns and superior in number of crew.

And there was more good news at sea. There were two holes left in the blockade by which blockade runners could slip in to carry goods to the faltering Confederacy. One was at Fort Fisher, North Carolina, the other at Mobile Bay, Alabama. For Mobile Bay, old salt Farragut was called in once again. Against him was a channel full of mines (torpedoes, they called them in those days) and the usual forts. Farragut went in, his gunners (left) at battle stations. The monitor Tecumsah hit a torpedo and sank; Farragut yelled "Damn the torpedoes! Full speed ahead!" They sailed past the forts. The Rebel Tennessee came out and a monitor hammered her into surrender. The Confederacy had exactly one port left. Lincoln wrote to his prized old salt:

The national thanks are tendered by the President to Admiral Farragut and Major General Canby for the skill and harmony with which the recent operations into Mobile Harbor . . . were planned and carried into execution.

*Uncle Billy Sherman's boys (above)
were in front of Atlanta and nothing
was surer than that John Hood would
be coming out to fight them. The
Texan tried to get around Sherman's
flank north of the city; he gained
nothing and lost men. Still,
Sherman couldn't get in; the lines
were too strong. Uncle Billy
left a screen and moved the bulk of
his force south to cut off Hood's*

railroad. Hood pulled out and Sherman sent Lincoln: "Atlanta is ours and fairly won." Lincoln sent him back:

The national thanks are herewith tendered by the President to Major General William T. Sherman and the gallant officers and soldiers of his command before Atlanta, for the distinguished ability, courage and perseverance displayed in the campaign in Georgia which . . . has resulted in the capture of the city of Atlanta.

Atlanta (below) was his. Sherman was now free to repeat Grant's gambit: to cut loose from his supply line and march to the sea. He set out to "make Georgia howl." There was nothing much in front of him; he was able to send the President Savannah for a Christ-

mas present. Lincoln sent him:

When you were about leaving Atlanta for
the Atlantic coast, I was anxious, if not
fearful, but feeling that you were the
better judge, and remembering that
"nothing risked, nothing gained" I did
not interfere. Now the undertaking
being a success, the honor is all yours.

It had been easier to get in front of Petersburg than take the place. Grant was there, but the stubborn, weary and hungry Confederates held on inside their fortifications. He settled down to siege (right) and once more, Lincoln backed him all the way:

I have seen your despatch expressing your unwillingness to break your hold where you are. Neither am I willing. Hold on with a bull-dog grip, and chew & choke, as much as possible.

To break the ring around Petersburg, there was a scheme for a regiment of Pennsylvania miners to dig a tunnel into the line, fill it with gun powder and blow the whole thing to blazes. They dug, the powder was laid and the mine went up. The result was a wasteland like the surface of the moon (right); but the follow-up assault was under none other than Burnside of Fredericksburg fame, and the result was a bungled affair which went so slowly that the shaken Confederates were able to get themselves reorganized and toss the stormers out of their lines with heavy casualties.

*Lee had one more wriggle left: the
old trick from McClellan's Peninsula
campaign—to threaten Washington with
a force in the Shenandoah Valley.
Jackson was gone; General Jubal Early
was sent to do the job and he gave
Lincoln a bad case of trembles.
He sent Grant a most urgent message:*

Now what I think is that you should pro-
vide to retain your hold where you are
certainly, and bring the rest with
you personally, and make a vigorous effort
to destroy the enemy's force in this
vicinity. I think there is really a fair
chance to do this if the movement
if prompt. This is what I think, upon
your suggestion, and it is not an order.

*Very well—no order. Instead of
coming himself, Grant sent General
Phil Sheridan (left, seated center).
Lincoln seemed well pleased:*

I have seen your despatch in which you say
''I want Sheridan put in command of all
the troops in the field, with instructions
to put himself South of the enemy
and follow him to the death. Wherever
the enemy goes, let our troops go
also.'' This, I think, is exactly right.

*In September, Sheridan came up
against Early at Winchester, Virginia,
and while his infantry pinned the
Confederate line, his cavalry—with
wild young horsemen like George Custer
(left) who would die later at Little
Big Horn—swept around the flank
and sent the Southerners running as
no Yankee had ever seen them run
before. Near Fisher's Hill, Early
stood and again Sheridan flanked him
out of the position. Lincoln wired:*

Have just heard of your great victory. God
bless you all, officers and men.
Strongly inclined to come and see you.

---

*Early made one more attack. It went
well at first, but Sheridan came gal-
loping up from twenty miles back of
the line to rally his men and win.
The Shenandoah was now out of the war.*

The elections were coming on, Petersburg still held out and Lincoln (right) had serious doubts as to whether a war weary nation would re-elect him. He wrote himself a memo:

This morning, as for some days past, it seems exceedingly probable that this Administration will not be re-elected. Then it will be my duty to so co-operate with the President-elect, as to save the Union between the election and the inauguration; as he will have secured his election on such ground that he cannot possibly save it afterwards.

The President could have saved his worry. Grant might be stalled, but the victories of Sherman and Sheridan swept him back for a second term.

Grant held Lee at Petersburg, Sher-
man harried a pitiful little force
now back under Joe Johnston in
the South. There was still one more
Confederate outfit, though, the army
John Hood (left) had led from Atlanta.
This impetuous Texan was now push-
ing up towards Nashville, Tennes-
see. There stood Thomas, "The Rock
of Chickamauga." "Old Slow Trot" they
called him in the service—and he
drove both Grant and Lincoln nearly
to fits by not attacking until he
was absolutely ready. When he did at-
tack over cold December fields, it
was a two day battle, then a rout
with Confederates flying south,
no longer an army. Thomas followed
the pursuit and his cavalry com-
mander James Wilson heard him calling
out of the dark, "Dang it to hell,
Wilson, didn't I tell you we could
lick 'em, didn't I tell you we could
lick 'em?" Lincoln congratulated him:

Please accept for yourselves, officers
and men, the nation's thanks for your
good work of yesterday. You made a magnificent beginning. A grand consummation is
within your easy reach. Do not let it slip.

For the shrinking South, there was
still one window on the world—Fort
Fisher at Wilmington, North Carolina.
Porter took the largest fleet the
United States had ever assembled
(above) to bombard it, then sent
infantry ashore.
A happy Lincoln said:

Sir: It is my agreeable duty to enclose
herewith a joint resolution approved 24th
January, 1865, tendering the thanks
of Congress to yourself, the officers
and men under your command, for their gallantry and good conduct in the capture
of Fort Fisher, and through you to all
who participated in that brilliant
and decisive victory under your command.

It was March and the war was clearly drawing to an end. As Lincoln stood before the Capitol (left) to deliver his Inaugural Address, he tried to face the nation toward the task of making peace which lay ahead:

... with malice toward none; with charity for all; with firmness in the right, as God gives us to see the right, let us strive on to finish the work we are in; to bind up the nation's wounds; to care for him who shall have borne the battle, and for his widow and his orphan —to do all which may achieve and cherish a just and a lasting peace, among ourselves, and with all nations.

195

*Lee's men in the Petersburg lines
were so few and so hungry. Grant extended a flank and they had to extend
to cover him—then suddenly, they
were extended too far and the Union
men were pouring through all along
the line. Petersburg fell, then
Richmond (below), flaming in an ac-
cidental fire. Lincoln wrote Grant:*

**Gen. Sheridan says ''If the thing is
pressed I think that Lee will surrender.''
Let the thing be pressed.**

The thing was pressed. Hard marching Yankees raced along Lee's flank to get across his line of retreat. It could be only hours before there was no more war, no more dead boys, no more letters from Lincoln to heart-broken women like Mrs. Bixby:

Dear Madame—I have just been shown in the files of the War Department a statement of the Adjutant General of Massachusetts, that you are the mother of five sons who have died gloriously on the field of battle. I feel how weak and fruitless must be any words of mine which should attempt to beguile you from the grief of a loss so overwhelming. But I cannot refrain from tendering to you the consolation that may be found in the thanks of the Republic they died to save.

I pray that our Heavenly Father may assuage the anguish of your bereavement and leave you only the cherished memory of the loved and lost, and the solemn pride that must be yours, to have laid so costly a sacrifice upon the altar of Freedom.

Lee's men trudged west and at Appomattox Court House they found Union troops ahead of them. The government of the Confederacy was in flight; the last army was starving and in rags. They had done all men could do and Lee did the only thing left to do. He and Grant met in the home of a Mr. McClean (below) and the war was over. Lincoln sent a message to the War Department for his son, Tad:

Tad wants some flags. Can he be accommodated?

We meet this evening, not in sorrow, but
in gladness of heart. The evacuation
of Petersburg and Richmond and the surrender of the principal insurgent army
give hope of a righteous and speedy peace.

The army shot Booth (left) as he hid
in a barn. Four more of the con-
spirators (left, from the top)—Mary
Surratt, Lewis Payne, George Atze-
rodt and David Herald—were hung
(above) at Washington Penitentiary.

The poet Walt Whitman gave words
to the nation's grief as a funeral
train (right) carried Lincoln
to rest at Springfield, Illinois:

•

Coffin that passes through lanes and
streets,
Through day and night with the great
cloud darkening the land,
With the pomp of the inloop'd flags
with the cities draped in black,
With the show of the States themselves as of crape-veil'd
women standing,
With processions long and winding and
the flambeaus of the night,
With the countless torches lit, with
the silent seas of faces and the
unbared heads,
With the waiting depot, the arriving
coffin and the sombre faces,
With dirges through the night, with
the thousand voices rising strong
and solemn,
With all the mournful voices of the
dirges pour'd around the coffin,
The dim-lit churches and the shudder-
ing organs—where amid these
you journey,
With the tolling tolling bell's perpetual clang,
Here, coffin that slowly passes,
I give you my sprig of lilac.

The Southerners went home and Grant
had let those who had horses keep them
to help get in a spring crop. The
victorious Northerners paraded
in Washington (right)—the eastern
men whom the Confederates had once
despised as "clerks" and the western
farmers who had marched with Sherman. It was all over now; the Union
was one and a man who was there
when Lee surrendered wrote, ". . . it
was felt by all that peace had
at last dawned upon the land. The
charges were now withdrawn from
the guns, the campfires were left
to smoulder in their ashes, the
flags were tenderly furled . . . and the
Army of the Union and the Army of
Northern Virginia turned their
backs upon each other for the first
time in four long, bloody years."
A private had summed it up earlier
for the soldiers: "Death is the common
lot of all and the difference between
dying to day and to morrow is
not much, but we all prefer to morrow."

Scale in Yards
0 — 2000

EWELL
OAK HILL

Gettysburg

MUMMASBURG ROAD

Willoughby

HARRISBURG ROAD

HUNTERSTOWN ROAD

A. P. HILL

SCHURZ

Rock

Railroad

YORK PIKE

Hanover

CHAMBERSBURG PIKE

HANOVER ROAD

Run

Gettysburg

HOWARD

CULP'S HILL

CEMETERY HILL

THE BATTLE OF GETTYSBURG
2:30 P.M., JULY 1, 1863

MUMMASBURG ROAD

EWELL

YORK PIKE

Mc Pherson's Woods

Gettysburg

HANOVER ROAD

Run

A. P. HILL

SEMINARY RIDGE

HAGERSTOWN ROAD

CEMETERY HILL

CULP'S HILL

WOLF HILL

HOWARD

Spangler's Springs

Benner's

BALTIMORE

Wheat Field

CEMETERY RIDGE

TANEYTOWN ROAD

Peach Orchard

LONGSTREET

SYKES

PIKE

Devil's Den

■ Federal forces
▨ Confederate forces
⚔ BATTLE SITES

LITTLE ROUND TOP

ROUND TOP

THE BATTLE OF GETTYSBURG
SHORTLY AFTER DARK, JULY 2, 1863

THE BATTLE OF GETTYSBURG
2:30 P. M., JULY 3, 1863
BEFORE CONFEDERATE ATTACK

OAK HILL

MUMMASBURG ROAD

Gettysburg

Run

CHAMBERSBURG PIKE

Hanover

EWELL

McPherson's Woods

Railroad

YORK

HANOVER

Rock Creek

HARRISBURG ROAD

HUNTERSTOWN PIKE

A. P. HILL

HAGERSTOWN ROAD

Gettysburg

LEE

SEMINARY RIDGE

580

Willoughby

Pickett

LONGSTREET

CULP'S HILL 620

CEMETERY HILL 620

GIBBON

SLOCUM

Benner's

WOLF HILL 672

Spangler's Springs

Doubleday

CEMETERY RIDGE

TANEYTOWN

MEADE

BALTIMORE PIKE

Rock Creek

Peach Orchard
McLaws

V I R G I N I A

SICKLES

Wheat Field 537

Devil's Den

LITTLE ROUND TOP 650

SYKES

ROUND TOP 785

Creek

EMMITSBURG ROAD

ROAD

Run

Run

Federal forces
Confederate forces

BATTLE SITES

Scale in Yards

0   2000

McD

ABOUT THE PHOTOGRAPHER

Most of the photographs in this book were made by Mathew Brady (right) or by photographers working for him. Born in upstate New York about 1823, Brady came to the city as a young man and first learned photography from lectures given by Samuel F. B. Morse, the famous inventor. Morse had seen Daguerreotypes made in France. Brady was only 21 when he opened his own studio at Broadway and Fulton Street. Ingeniously experimenting with skylights in the roof and with reflectors, the young man became the city's leading portrait photographer. Even so early, his journalist's instinct led him to attempt to make a complete photographic record of all the notables of his day. To this end, he opened a second gallery in Washington.

When the war came, it seemed to release some deep instinct in the man. He said later, "I felt that I had to go—and I went." Neglecting his studio practice, he took the field with

the troops and when the task became too great for one man, hired assistants to cover areas he could not reach personally. Two of his assistants, Alexander Gardner and Timothy O'Sullivan, became famous in their own right.

The work involved in their pictures was remarkably complicated. The most advanced process was the wet collodion plate. A chemical mixture was first poured on a glass plate. The plate was then sensitized in a mixture of water and silver nitrate and placed in the camera still wet. The exposure was then made and the plate rushed immediately to the wagon dark room (right) for developing. Plates were often as large as a shirt cardboard.

An active collaborator in the venture was Edward Anthony, the photographic supply dealer whose firm eventually became the Ansco Company. Anthony allowed Brady large credits for equipment when his own resources proved unequal to the task. After the war, when Brady ran into serious financial difficulties, he sold one set of his negatives to Anthony. This set was eventually placed in the Library of Congress. A second set was purchased by the government and is now cared for in the National Archives. A final group of plates were found recently in Oswego, New York. Ansco—which kindly supplied many of the prints for this book—acquired these and now has them in the National Archives for safekeeping.

Brady was not the first war correspondent with a camera; Roger Fenton had earlier made pictures of the Crimean conflict. No one previously, however, had attempted to cover an entire war and certainly no single photographer has ever covered a war better. His portraits of the leaders and men are unsurpassed and many of his scenes could not be improved upon today by men working with the most modern equipment. No photographer has ever left a body of work of such magnificent quality and historical interest.

A NOTE ON THE PICTURES

The photographs in this book were all
reproduced from original glass-plate
negatives either by direct contact
printing or from copy negatives. In one
or two cases, where the original plates
were lost or destroyed, the reproduction
was made from an early printed copy
or a carte-de-visite sepia positive.
While some of the pictures have been
cropped for visual effect, as an aid to
design, every effort has been made to
preserve the flavor of these 100-year-old
negatives: water-damaged emulsions,
breaks, cracks or chips in the glass
negatives, tones faded by age, and
scratches or bruises in the too-frequently
handled plate surfaces have all been
preserved as they appear in the
negatives now stored carefully in
Washington.

PICTURE SOURCES

There are two great Brady Collections.
One is at the National Archives, the
other at the Library of Congress. Both
are in Washington, D. C. Anyone may
visit either collection and prints are
available for a nominal charge. Both
have microfilm records of their
Brady Collections which are available

for $6.00 and $7.50. The pictures which
are not credited below come from the
author's personal collection, but the
great majority of them are available
from either the Archives or the Library.

THE NATIONAL ARCHIVES, Washington, D.C.:
pp. 16, 18, 19, 23, 26-7, 28-9, 33 (top),
34-5, 36, 39, 48-9, 50-1, 62-3, 64-5, 66,
68-9, 73, 81, 84-5, 88, 90-1, 92-3, 94-5,
96-7, 98-9, 101, 107, 109, 110-1, 112-3,
114, 118-9, 121, 125, 127, 136-7, 138-9,
140-1, 142-3, 144, 147, 148-9, 154-5, 156,

158-9, 167, 168-9, 170-1, 172, 174-5, 176-7,
181, 182, 194-5, 200, 201 (top).

THE LIBRARY OF CONGRESS, Washington, D.C.:
pp. 52-3, 59, 76-7, 128-9, 160-1, 219.

CULVER SERVICE, New York, N. Y.:
pp. 14-5, 20-1, 33 (bottom), 45, 47, 71, 75,
145, 163, 165, 187, 188, 204-5, 206

THE BETTMANN ARCHIVE, New York, N. Y.:
pp. 102-3

THE VALENTINE MUSEUM, Richmond, Virginia:
pp. 24-5 (By George S. Cook.)

THE NATIONAL PARK SERVICE, Washington, D.C.:
pp. 132-135. (These paintings are details from
the Gettysburg Cyclorama by Paul Philippoteaux.)

ANSCO HISTORICAL COLLECTION, Binghamton, N. Y.:
pp. 152.

IN WORDS AND PICTURES

Bantam introduces three unique books dealing with important events and figures in America's history. Each book gains added dimension through the combination of important words from speeches, letters and news reports—together with fine illustrations via photographs, engravings, cartoons, paintings. Each book is a new and exciting reading experience.

•

THE CIVIL WAR AS THEY KNEW IT (SP134 • 75¢) The Civil War comes to life through the combination of Abraham Lincoln's important words and Mathew Brady's striking photographs. This year-by-year account of the historic conflict includes Lincoln's notable comments, writings and speeches matched with on-the-spot war photographs by Brady, the first photographer to cover an entire war. Edited by Pierce G. Fredericks.

THE YANKS ARE COMING (SP136 • 75¢) The total experience of World War I as detailed through brilliant eye-witness descriptions by outstanding writers and reporters of that era. The illustrations include famous photographs and maps tracing every battle from 1914 through 1918. Compiled and edited by Pierce G. Fredericks.

PRESIDENTS OF THE U.S.A.: PROFILES AND PICTURES (SP135 • 75¢) In one up-to-date volume, here are illustrated biographies of the nation's chief executives from George Washington to Lyndon Johnson. There are important facts and statistics as well as anecdote-filled profiles of each president. These are matched with hundreds of rare prints, paintings, political cartoons and family snapshots to create a rounded portrait of each president. Edited by Cornel Adam Lengyel.

AVAILABLE AT NEWSSTANDS EVERYWHERE